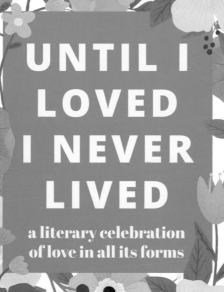

UNTIL I
LOVED
I NEVER
LIVED

a literary celebration
of love in all its forms

An Hachette UK Company
www.hachette.co.uk

First published in Great Britain in 2022 by Pyramid,
an imprint of Octopus Publishing Group Ltd
Carmelite House, 50 Victoria Embankment,
London EC4Y 0DZ
www.octopusbooks.co.uk

Distributed in the US by
Hachette Book Group
1290 Avenue of the Americas
4th and 5th Floors
New York, NY 10104

Distributed in Canada by
Canadian Manda Group
664 Annette St.
Toronto, Ontario, Canada M6S 2C8

ISBN 978-0-75373-495-7

A CIP catalogue record for this book is available
from the British Library

Printed and bound in China

10 9 8 7 6 5 4 3 2 1

INTRODUCTION

Whether it's the joy, confusion or agony of love – or whether it's the love you have for your partner, friends, family or even a stranger – we've all experienced love in some way or another. And who better to capture everything that love encompasses than the greatest writers in history?

From the poets of the Romantic era, such as Wordsworth and Byron, to the great Victorian novelists, such as the Brontës and Dickens, the concept of love in all its forms has been a hallmark of literature throughout the ages. Whose heart doesn't ache at Heathcliffe's and Catherine's all-consuming love for each other? And who doesn't hold their breath during Gatsby's and Daisy's tense reunion? Who can resist a monologue in which a character declares their undying love for someone, or a sonnet that conveys love's deepest sorrows in fourteen impassioned lines?

Whatever your experience of love, this beautiful collection of quotes from across literature is a celebration of one of life's most powerful and intensely felt emotions. Read it from cover to cover, or dip into it whenever you want; keep it on your bookshelf or pass it on to a loved one when you've finished reading. And – most importantly – take comfort in knowing that, whatever love has thrown your way, you will find all the solace you need in these pages.

What the world stigmatizes as romantic is often more nearly allied to the truth than is commonly supposed.

ANNE BRONTË

SONNET 18

Shall I compare thee to a summer's day?
Thou art more lovely and more temperate:
Rough winds do shake the darling buds of May,
And summer's lease hath all too short a date;
Sometime too hot the eye of heaven shines,
And often is his gold complexion dimm'd;
And every fair from fair sometime declines,
By chance or nature's changing course untrimm'd;
But thy eternal summer shall not fade,
Nor lose possession of that fair thou ow'st;
Nor shall death brag thou wander'st in his shade,
When in eternal lines to time thou grow'st:
So long as men can breathe or eyes can see,
So long lives this, and this gives life to thee.

WILLIAM SHAKESPEARE

The Passionate Shepherd to His Love

Come live with me and be my love,
And we will all the pleasures prove,
That Valleys, groves, hills, and fields,
Woods, or steepy mountain yields.

And we will sit upon the Rocks,
Seeing the Shepherds feed their flocks,
By shallow Rivers to whose falls
Melodious birds sing Madrigals.

And I will make thee beds of Roses
And a thousand fragrant posies,
A cap of flowers, and a kirtle
Embroidered all with leaves of Myrtle;

A gown made of the finest wool

Which from our pretty Lambs we pull;

Fair lined slippers for the cold,

With buckles of the purest gold;

A belt of straw and Ivy buds,

With Coral clasps and Amber studs:

And if these pleasures may thee move,

Come live with me, and be my love.

The Shepherds' Swains shall dance and sing

For thy delight each May-morning:

If these delights thy mind may move,

Then live with me, and be my love.

CHRISTOPHER MARLOWE

I have been astonished that Men could die Martyrs for religion – I have shudder'd at it – I shudder no more. I could be martyr'd for my Religion – Love is my religion – I could die for that. I could die for you. My Creed is Love and you are its only tenet.

John Keats

How do I Love thee?

How do I love thee? Let me count the ways.
I love thee to the depth and breadth and height
My soul can reach, when feeling out of sight
For the ends of being and ideal grace.
I love thee to the level of every day's
Most quiet need, by sun and candle-light.
I love thee freely, as men strive for right;
I love thee purely, as they turn from praise.
I love thee with the passion put to use
In my old griefs, and with my childhood's faith.
I love thee with a love I seemed to lose
With my lost saints. I love thee with the breath,
Smiles, tears, of all my life; and, if God choose,
I shall but love thee better after death.

Elizabeth Barrett Browning

Amoretti LXXV: One Day I Wrote Her Name

One day I wrote her name upon the strand,

But came the waves and washed it away:

Again I wrote it with a second hand,

But came the tide, and made my pains his prey.

"Vain man," said she, "that dost in vain assay,

A mortal thing so to immortalize;

For I myself shall like to this decay,

And eke my name be wiped out likewise."

"Not so," (quod I) "let baser things devise

To die in dust, but you shall live by fame:

My verse your vertues rare shall eternize,

And in the heavens write your glorious name:

Where whenas death shall all the world subdue,

Our love shall live, and later life renew."

Edmund Spenser

And ever has it been that love knows not its own depth until the hour of separation.

The Coming of the Ship, Kahlil Gibran

If music be the food of love, play on.

Twelfth Night, William Shakespeare

I have for the first time found what I can truly love – I have found you. You are my sympathy – my better self – my good angel – I am bound to you with a strong attachment. I think you good, gifted, lovely: a fervent, a solemn passion is conceived in my heart; it leans to you, draws you to my centre and spring of life, wrap my existence about you – and, kindling in pure, powerful flame, fuses you and me in one.

JANE EYRE, CHARLOTTE BRONTË

Take, Oh, Take Those Lips Away

Take, oh, take those lips away
That so sweetly were forsworn
And those eyes, like break of day,
Lights that do mislead the morn;
But my kisses bring again,
Seals of love, though sealed in vain.

Hide, oh, hide those hills of snow,
Which thy frozen bosom bears,
On whose tops the pinks that grow
Are of those that April wears;
But first set my poor heart free,
Bound in those icy chains by thee.

John Fletcher

There is nothing I would not do for those who are really my friends. I have no notion of loving people by halves, it is not my nature.

Northanger Abbey, Jane Austen

First Love

I ne'er was struck before that hour
With love so sudden and so sweet,
Her face it bloomed like a sweet flower
And stole my heart away complete.
My face turned pale as deadly pale,
My legs refused to walk away,
And when she looked, what could I ail?
My life and all seemed turned to clay.

And then my blood rushed to my face
And took my eyesight quite away,
The trees and bushes round the place
Seemed midnight at noonday.
I could not see a single thing,
Words from my eyes did start—
They spoke as chords do from the string,
And blood burnt round my heart.

Are flowers the winter's choice?
Is love's bed always snow?
She seemed to hear my silent voice,
Not love's appeals to know.
I never saw so sweet a face
As that I stood before.
My heart has left its dwelling-place
And can return no more.

JOHN CLARE

He accompanied her up the hill, explaining to her the details of his forthcoming tenure of the other farm. They spoke very little of their mutual feeling; pretty phrases and warm expressions being probably unnecessary between such tried friends. Theirs was that substantial affection which arises (if any arises at all) when the two who are thrown together begin first by knowing the rougher sides of each other's character, and not the best till further on, the romance growing up in the interstices of a mass of hard prosaic reality.

FAR FROM THE MADDING CROWD, THOMAS HARDY

They do not love that do not show their love.

The Two Gentleman of Verona,
William Shakespeare

Blessed is the influence of one true, loving human soul on another.

George Eliot

Mediocrity in Love Rejected

Give me more love or more disdain;
The torrid, or the frozen zone,
Bring equal ease unto my pain;
The temperate affords me none;
Either extreme, of love, or hate,
Is sweeter than a calm estate.

Give me a storm; if it be love,
Like Danae in that golden show'r
I swim in pleasure; if it prove
Disdain, that torrent will devour
My vulture-hopes; and he's possess'd
Of heaven, that's but from hell releas'd.

Then crown my joys, or cure my pain;
Give me more love, or more disdain.

Thomas Carew

The place where she stood seemed to him a holy shrine, unapproachable, and there was one moment when he was almost retreating, so overwhelmed was he with terror. He had to make an effort to master himself, and to remind himself that people of all sorts were moving about her, and that he too might come there to skate. He walked down, for a long while avoiding looking at her as at the sun, but seeing her, as one does the sun, without looking.

ANNA KARENINA, LEO TOLSTOY

He's more myself than I am.
Whatever our souls are made
of, his and mine are the same.

WUTHERING HEIGHTS, EMILY BRONTË

If I loved you less, I might be able to talk about it more.

EMMA, JANE AUSTEN

Sonnet 43

When most I wink, then do mine eyes best see,

For all the day they view things unrespected;

But when I sleep, in dreams they look on thee,

And darkly bright, are bright in dark directed.

Then thou, whose shadow shadows doth make bright,

How would thy shadow's form form happy show

To the clear day with thy much clearer light,

When to unseeing eyes thy shade shines so!

How would, I say, mine eyes be blessed made

By looking on thee in the living day,

When in dead night thy fair imperfect shade

Through heavy sleep on sightless eyes doth stay!

All days are nights to see till I see thee,

And nights bright days when dreams do show thee me.

William Shakespeare

You anticipate what I would say, though you cannot know how earnestly I say it, how earnestly I feel it, without knowing my secret heart, and the hopes and fears and anxieties with which it has long been laden. Dear Doctor Manette, I love your daughter fondly, dearly, disinterestedly, devotedly. If ever there were love in the world, I love her. You have loved yourself; let your old love speak for me!

A Tale of Two Cities, Charles Dickens

My heart is too thoroughly dried to be broken in a hurry, and I mean to live as long as I can.

The Tenant of Wildfell Hall, Anne Brontë

Love's Philosophy

The fountains mingle with the river,
And the rivers with the ocean,
The winds of heaven mix forever
With a sweet emotion;
Nothing in the world is single;
All things by law divine
In one spirit meet and mingle.
Why not I with thine?—

See the mountains kiss high heaven
And the waves clasp one another;
No sister-flower would be forgiven
If it disdained its brother;
And sunlight clasps the earth
And the moonbeams kiss the sea:
What is all this sweet work worth
If thou kiss not me?

Percy Bysshe Shelley

May be we are not such fools as we look. But though we be, we are well content, so long as we may be two fools together.

LORNA DOONE, R.D. BLACKMORE

You pierce my soul. I am half agony, half hope. Tell me not that I am too late, that such precious feelings are gone for ever. I offer myself to you again with a heart even more your own than when you almost broke it, eight years and a half ago. Dare not say that man forgets sooner than woman, that his love has an earlier death. I have loved none but you.

PERSUASION, JANE AUSTEN

For a friend with
an understanding
heart is worth
no less than a
brother.

THE ODYSSEY, HOMER

But that I know love is begun by time,
And that I see, in passages of proof,
Time qualifies the spark and fire of it.

HAMLET, WILLIAM SHAKESPEARE

"At first I did not love you, Jude; that I own. When I first knew you I merely wanted you to love me. I did not exactly flirt with you; but that inborn craving which undermines some women's morals almost more than unbridled passion – the craving to attract and captivate, regardless of the injury it may do the man – was in me; and when I found I had caught you, I was frightened. And then – I don't know how it was – I couldn't bear to let you go – possibly to Arabella again – and so I got to love you, Jude. But you see, however fondly it ended, it began in the selfish and cruel wish to make your heart ache for me without letting mine ache for you."

JUDE THE OBSCURE, THOMAS HARDY

To My Dear and Loving Husband

If ever two were one, then surely we.

If ever man were loved by wife, then thee.

If ever wife was happy in a man,

Compare with me, ye women, if you can.

I prize thy love more than whole mines of gold,

Or all the riches that the East doth hold.

My love is such that rivers cannot quench,

Nor ought but love from thee give recompense.

Thy love is such I can no way repay;

The heavens reward thee manifold, I pray.

Then while we live, in love let's so persever,

That when we live no more, we may live ever.

Anne Bradstreet

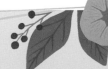

You can love a person dear to you with a human love, but an enemy can only be loved with divine love.

War and Peace, Leo Tolstoy

Even where the affections are not strongly moved by any superior excellence, the companions of our childhood always possess a certain power over our minds, which hardly any later friend can obtain. They know our infantine dispositions, which, however they may be afterwards modified, are never eradicated; and they can judge of our actions with more certain conclusions as to the integrity of our motives.

Frankenstein, Mary Wollstonecraft Shelley

For my part,
I prefer my heart
to be broken.
It is so lovely,
dawn-kaleidoscopic
within the crack.

POMEGRANATE, D.H. LAWRENCE

I Gave Myself to Him

I gave myself to Him –
And took Himself, for Pay,
The solemn contract of a Life
Was ratified, this way –

The Wealth might disappoint –
Myself a poorer prove
Than this great Purchaser suspect,
The Daily Own – of Love

Depreciate the Vision –
But till the Merchant buy –
Still Fable – in the Isles of Spice –
The subtle Cargoes – lie –

At least – 'tis Mutual – Risk –
Some – found it – Mutual Gain –
Sweet Debt of Life – Each Night to owe –
Insolvent – every Noon –

EMILY DICKINSON

**Do but look on her eyes;
they do light
All that Love's world
compriseth!**

HER TRIUMPH, BEN JONSON

"Are people so unhappy when they love?"
"Yes, Christine, when they love and are not sure of being loved."

The Phantom of the Opera, Gaston Leroux

As to Emma, she did not ask herself whether she loved. Love, she thought, must come suddenly, with great outbursts and lightnings — a hurricane of the skies, which falls upon life, revolutionises it, roots up the will like a leaf, and sweeps the whole heart into the abyss. She did not know that on the terrace of houses it makes lakes when the pipes are choked, and she would thus have remained in her security when she suddenly discovered a rent in the wall of it.

MADAME BOVARY, GUSTAVE FLAUBERT

Why should you
love him whom the
world hates so?
Because he love
me more than all
the world.

Edward II, Christopher Marlowe

"Marriage is so unlike everything else. There is something even awful in the nearness it brings. Even if we loved someone else better than—than those we were married to, it would be no use"—poor Dorothea, in her palpitating anxiety, could only seize her language brokenly—"I mean, marriage drinks up all our power of giving or getting any blessedness in that sort of love. I know it may be very dear—but it murders our marriage—and then the marriage stays with us like a murder—and everything else is gone. And then our husband—if he loved and trusted us, and we have not helped him, but made a curse in his life—"

Middlemarch, George Eliot

Well, you never knew exactly how much space you occupied in people's lives. Yet from this fog his affection emerged – the best contacts are when one knows the obstacles and still wants to preserve a relation.

Tender is the Night, F. Scott Fitzgerald

A Sonnet to the Noble Lady, the Lady Mary Wroth

I that have been a lover, and could show it,

Though not in these, in rithmes not wholly dumb,

Since I exscribe your sonnets, am become

A better lover, and much better poet.

Nor is my Muse or I ashamed to owe it

To those true numerous graces, whereof some

But charm the senses, others overcome

Both brains and hearts; and mine now best do know it:

For in your verse all Cupid's armory,

His flames, his shafts, his quiver, and his bow,

His very eyes are yours to overthrow.

But then his mother's sweets you so apply,

Her joys, her smiles, her loves, as readers take

For Venus' ceston every line you make.

Ben Jonson

But nothing is
so strange when
one is in love ...
as the complete
indifference of
other people.

Mrs Dalloway, Virginia Woolf

from Platonic Love

Indeed I must confess,

When souls mix 'tis an happiness,

But not complete till bodies too do join,

And both our wholes into one whole combine;

But half of heaven the souls in glory taste

Till by love in heaven at last

Their bodies too are placed.

In thy immortal part

Man, as well as I, thou art.

But something 'tis that differs thee and me,

And we must one even in that difference be.

I thee both as a man and woman prize,

For a perfect love implies

Love in all capacities.

ABRAHAM COWLEY

from The Definition of Love

My love is of a birth as rare
As 'tis for object strange and high;
It was begotten by Despair
Upon Impossibility.

Magnanimous Despair alone
Could show me so divine a thing
Where feeble Hope could ne'er have flown,
But vainly flapp'd its tinsel wing.

And yet I quickly might arrive
Where my extended soul is fixt,
But Fate does iron wedges drive,
And always crowds itself betwixt.

For Fate with jealous eye does see
Two perfect loves, nor lets them close;
Their union would her ruin be,
And her tyrannic pow'r depose.

Andrew Marvell

But we loved with a love that
was more than love—
I and my Annabel Lee—
With a love that the wingéd
seraphs of Heaven
Coveted her and me.

Annabel Lee, Edgar Allan Poe

She makes me love her and I like people who make me love them. It saves me so much trouble making myself love them.

Anne of Green Gables, L.M. Montgomery

Gatsby believed in the green light, the orgastic future that year by year recedes before us. It eluded us then, but that's no matter—tomorrow we will run faster, stretch out our arms farther... And one fine morning— So we beat on, boats against the current, borne back ceaselessly into the past.

THE GREAT GATSBY, F. SCOTT FITZGERALD

A Red, Red Rose

O my Luve is like a red, red rose
That's newly sprung in June;
O my Luve is like the melody
That's sweetly played in tune.

So fair art thou, my bonnie lass,
So deep in luve am I;
And I will luve thee still, my dear,
Till a' the seas gang dry.

Till a' the seas gang dry, my dear,
And the rocks melt wi' the sun;
I will love thee still, my dear,
While the sands o' life shall run.

And fare thee weel, my only luve!
And fare thee weel awhile!
And I will come again, my luve,
Though it were ten thousand mile.

Robert Burns

Each time you happen to
me all over again.

The Age of Innocence, Edith Wharton

Her affection for him was now the breath and life of Tess's being; it enveloped her as a photosphere, irradiated her into forgetfulness of her past sorrows, keeping back the gloomy spectres that would persist in their attempts to touch her—doubt, fear, moodiness, care, shame. She knew that they were waiting like wolves just outside the circumscribing light, but she had long spells of power to keep them in hungry subjection there.

TESS OF THE D'URBERVILLES, THOMAS HARDY

Love her, love her, love her!
If she favours you, love her.
If she wounds you, love her.
If she tears your heart to
pieces – and as it gets older
and stronger, it will tear
deeper – love her, love
her, love her!

GREAT EXPECTATIONS, CHARLES DICKENS

What Is Love? I have met in the streets a very poor young man who was in love. His hat was old, his coat worn, the water passed through his shoes and the stars through his soul.

Les Misérables, Victor Hugo

The Secret

I loved thee, though I told thee not,
Right earlily and long,
Thou wert my joy in every spot,
My theme in every song.
And when I saw a stranger face
Where beauty held the claim,
I gave it like a secret grace
The being of thy name.
And all the charms of face or voice
Which I in others see
Are but the recollected choice
Of what I felt for thee.

John Clare

To love and win is the best thing. To love and lose, the next best.

The History of Pendennis,
William Makepeace Thackeray

Friendship between Ephelia and Ardelia

Eph. What Friendship is, Ardelia show.

Ard. 'Tis to love, as I love you.

Eph. This account, so short (tho' kind)

Suits not my inquiring mind.

Therefore farther now repeat:

What is Friendship when complete?

Ard. 'Tis to share all joy and grief;

'Tis to lend all due relief

From the tongue, the heart, the hand;

'Tis to mortgage house and land;

For a friend be sold a slave;

'Tis to die upon a grave,

If a friend therein do lie.

Eph. This indeed, tho' carried high,

This, tho' more than e'er was done

Underneath the rolling sun,

This has all been said before.

Can Ardelia say no more?

Ard. Words indeed no more can show:

But 'tis to love, as I love you.

Countess of Winchilsea Anne Finch

I loved her against reason, against promise, against peace, against hope, against happiness, against all discouragement that could be.

GREAT EXPECTATIONS, CHARLES DICKENS

"And now things have come to such a pass that, unless I can speak to you openly, I believe I shall go mad. I think of you as the most beautiful, the truest thing in the world," he continued, filled with a sense of exaltation, and feeling that he had no need now to choose his words with pedantic accuracy, for what he wanted to say was suddenly become plain to him.

"I see you everywhere, in the stars, in the river; to me you're everything that exists; the reality of everything. Life, I tell you, would be impossible without you…"

NIGHT AND DAY, VIRGINIA WOOLF

The Garden of Love

I went to the Garden of Love,

And saw what I never had seen:

A Chapel was built in the midst,

Where I used to play on the green.

And the gates of this Chapel were shut,

And 'Thou shalt not' writ over the door;

So I turn'd to the Garden of Love,

That so many sweet flowers bore.

And I saw it was filled with graves,

And tomb-stones where flowers should be:

And Priests in black gowns, were walking their rounds,

And binding with briars, my joys & desires.

William Blake

Be worthy of love, and love will come.

LITTLE WOMEN, LOUISA MAY ALCOTT

A Golden Day

I found you and I lost you,
All on a gleaming day.
The day was filled with sunshine,
And the land was full of May.

A golden bird was singing
Its melody divine,
I found you and I loved you,
And all the world was mine.

I found you and I lost you,
All on a golden day,
But when I dream of you, dear,
It is always brimming May.

PAUL LAURENCE DUNBAR

I have not broken your heart – you have broken it; and in breaking it, you have broken mine.

WUTHERING HEIGHTS, EMILY BRONTË

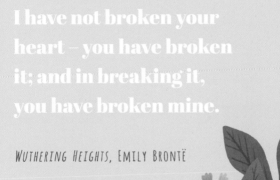

The difference between love and respect was markedly shown in her conduct. Bathsheba had spoken of her interest in Boldwood with the greatest freedom to Liddy, but she had only communed with her own heart concerning Troy.

All this infatuation Gabriel saw, and was troubled thereby from the time of his daily journey a-field to the time of his return, and on to the small hours of many a night. That he was not beloved had hitherto been his great sorrow; that Bathsheba was getting into the toils was now a sorrow greater than the first, and one which nearly obscured it. It was a result which paralleled the oft-quoted observation of Hippocrates concerning physical pains.

Far From the Madding Crowd, Thomas Hardy

Love will not be constrain'd by mastery.

When mast'ry comes, the god of love anon

Beateth his wings, and, farewell, he is gone.

Love is a thing as any spirit free.

The Canterbury Tales, Geoffrey Chaucer

I loved you first: but afterwards your love

I loved you first: but afterwards your love

Outsoaring mine, sang such a loftier song

As drowned the friendly cooings of my dove.

Which owes the other most? my love was long,

And yours one moment seemed to wax more strong;

I loved and guessed at you, you construed me

And loved me for what might or might not be –

Nay, weights and measures do us both a wrong.

For verily love knows not 'mine' or 'thine;'

With separate 'I' and 'thou' free love has done,

For one is both and both are one in love:

Rich love knows nought of 'thine that is not mine;'

Both have the strength and both the length thereof,

Both of us, of the love which makes us one.

Christina Rossetti

Never love anyone who treats you like you're ordinary.

Oscar Wilde

WHEN WE TWO PARTED

When we two parted
In silence and tears,
Half broken-hearted
To sever for years,
Pale grew thy cheek and cold,
Colder thy kiss;
Truly that hour foretold
Sorrow to this.

The dew of the morning
Sunk chill on my brow—
It felt like the warning
Of what I feel now.
Thy vows are all broken,
And light is thy fame;
I hear thy name spoken,
And share in its shame.

They name thee before me,
A knell to mine ear;
A shudder comes o'er me—
Why wert thou so dear?
They know not I knew thee,
Who knew thee too well—
Long, long shall I rue thee,
Too deeply to tell.

In secret we met—
In silence I grieve,
That thy heart could forget,
Thy spirit deceive.
If I should meet thee
After long years,
How should I greet thee?—
With silence and tears.

LORD BYRON

My love is selfish.

I cannot breathe without you.

JOHN KEATS

"When I talk of homes," pursued Nicholas, "I talk of mine – which is yours of course. If it were defined by any particular four walls and a roof, God knows I should be sufficiently puzzled to say whereabouts it lay; but that is not what I mean. When I speak of home, I speak of the place where – in default of a better – those I love are gathered together; and if that place were a gypsy's tent, or a barn, I should call it by the same name notwithstanding."

NICHOLAS NICKLEBY, CHARLES DICKENS

'Tis better to have
loved and lost than
never to have loved
at all.

*In Memoriam A.H.H.,
Alfred, Lord Tennyson*

The Sick Rose

O Rose thou art sick.

The invisible worm,

That flies in the night

In the howling storm:

Has found out thy bed

Of crimson joy:

And his dark secret love

Does thy life destroy.

William Blake

A Broken Appointment

You did not come,
And marching Time drew on, and wore me numb,
Yet less for loss of your dear presence there
Than that I thus found lacking in your make
That high compassion which can overbear
Reluctance for pure loving kindness' sake
Grieved I, when, as the hope-hour stroked its sum,
You did not come.

You love not me,
And love alone can lend you loyalty;
—I know and knew it. But, unto the store
Of human deeds divine in all but name,
Was it not worth a little hour or more
To add yet this: Once you, a woman, came
To soothe a time-torn man; even though it be
You love not me?

Thomas Hardy

If I can stop
one heart
from breaking,
I shall not live
in vain.

EMILY DICKINSON

He knew that when he kissed this girl, and forever wed his unutterable visions to her perishable breath, his mind would never romp again like the mind of God. So, he waited, listening for a moment longer to the tuning fork that had been struck upon a star. Then he kissed her. At his lips' touch she blossomed for him like a flower and the incarnation was complete.

The Great Gatsby, F. Scott Fitzgerald

I had not intended to love him; the reader knows I had wrought hard to extirpate from my soul the germs of love there detected; and now, at the first renewed view of him, they spontaneously revived, great and strong! He made me love him without looking at me.

Jane Eyre, Charlotte Brontë

Only in the agony of parting do we look into the depths of love.

FELIX HOLT, THE RADICAL, George Eliot

Elemental

Why don't people leave off being lovable
Or thinking they are lovable, or wanting to be lovable,
And be a bit elemental instead?

Since man is made up of the elements
Fire, and rain, and air, and live loam
And none of these is lovable
But elemental,
Man is lop-sided on the side of the angels.

I wish men would get back their balance among the elements
And be a bit more firey, as incapable of telling lies
As fire is.
I wish they'd be true to their own variation, as water is,
Which goes through all the stages of steam and stream and ice
Without losing its head.

I am sick of lovable people,
Somehow they are a lie.

D.H. Lawrence

"In vain have I struggled. It will not do. My feelings will not be repressed. You must allow me to tell you how ardently I admire and love you." Elizabeth's astonishment was beyond expression. She stared, coloured, doubted, and was silent. This he considered sufficient encouragement, and the avowal of all that he felt and had long felt for her, immediately followed.

PRIDE AND PREJUDICE, JANE AUSTEN

Years of love have
been forgot, in the
hatred of a minute.

The Complete Stories and Poems, Edgar Allan Poe

Sonnet 116

Let me not to the marriage of true minds

Admit impediments. Love is not love

Which alters when it alteration finds,

Or bends with the remover to remove.

O no! it is an ever-fixed mark

That looks on tempests and is never shaken;

It is the star to every wand'ring bark,

Whose worth's unknown, although his height be taken.

Love's not Time's fool, though rosy lips and cheeks

Within his bending sickle's compass come;

Love alters not with his brief hours and weeks,

But bears it out even to the edge of doom.

If this be error and upon me prov'd,

I never writ, nor no man ever lov'd.

William Shakespeare

Love has its own dark morality when rivalry enters in.

Jude the Obscure, Thomas Hardy

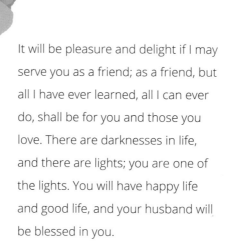

It will be pleasure and delight if I may serve you as a friend; as a friend, but all I have ever learned, all I can ever do, shall be for you and those you love. There are darknesses in life, and there are lights; you are one of the lights. You will have happy life and good life, and your husband will be blessed in you.

DRACULA, BRAM STOKER

Love is the
energy of life.

ROBERT BROWNING

He was in love, very much in love; and it was a love which, operating on an active, sanguine spirit, of more warmth than delicacy, made her affection appear of greater consequence, because it was withheld, and determined him to have the glory, as well as the felicity of forcing her to love him.

MANSFIELD PARK, JANE AUSTEN

The persons whom you cannot care for in a novel, because they are so bad, are the very same that you so dearly love in your life, because they are so good.

The Eustace Diamonds, Anthony Trollope

from Stella Maris

Why is it I remember yet
You, of all women one has met,
In random wayfare, as one meets
The chance romances of the streets,
The Juliet of a night? I know
Your heart holds many a Romeo.
And I, who call to mind your face
In so serene a pausing-place,
Where the bright pure expanse of sea,
Seems a reproach to you and me,
I too have sought on many a breast
The ecstasy of an unrest,
I too have had my dreams, and met

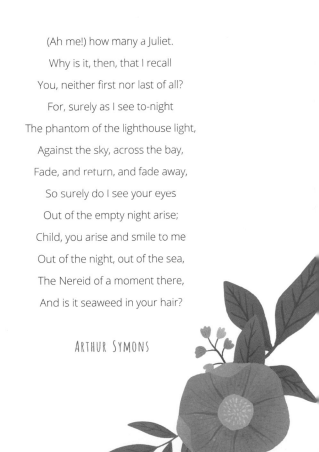

(Ah me!) how many a Juliet.

Why is it, then, that I recall

You, neither first nor last of all?

For, surely as I see to-night

The phantom of the lighthouse light,

Against the sky, across the bay,

Fade, and return, and fade away,

So surely do I see your eyes

Out of the empty night arise;

Child, you arise and smile to me

Out of the night, out of the sea,

The Nereid of a moment there,

And is it seaweed in your hair?

ARTHUR SYMONS

It lies not in our power to love or hate,

For will in us is overruled by fate.

When two are stripped, long ere the course begin,

We wish that one should lose, the other win;

And one especially do we affect

Of two gold ingots, like in each respect:

The reason no man knows; let it suffice

What we behold is censured by our eyes.

Where both deliberate, the love is slight:

Who ever loved, that loved not at first sight?

HERO AND LEANDER, CHRISTOPHER MARLOWE

To love oneself is the beginning of a lifelong romance.

An Ideal Husband, Oscar Wilde